HELLO BABY

HELLO BABY

A record book of milestones & memories in the first 12 months

CICO BOOKS
LONDON NEW YORK

Published in 2018 by CICO Books
An imprint of Ryland Peters & Small Ltd

20–21 Jockey's Fields
London WC1R 4BW

341 E 116th St
New York, NY 10029

www.rylandpeters.com

10 9 8 7 6 5 4 3 2

A CIP catalog record for this book is available from the Library of Congress and the British Library.

ISBN: 978 1 78249 665 6

Printed in China

Editor: Dawn Bates

Designer: Eliana Holder

Art director: Sally Powell

Production manager: Gordana Simakovic

Publishing manager: Penny Craig

Publisher: Cindy Richards

Contents

Welcome to the World 6
Welcome Home 8
Special Memories of Your First Weeks 10

Month-by-month Memories

1 month old 14
2 months old 15
3 months old 16
4 months old 17
5 months old 18
6 months old 19
7 months old 20
8 months old 21
9 months old 22
10 months old 23
11 months old 24
12 months old 25
Your Tiny Hands 26
Special Memories of the First Year 30

Special Firsts

It's Bathtime! 34
See You Later... 36
Say Cheese! 38
Time for Lunch? 40
On the Move... 42
You've Got Teeth 44
Stepping Out 46
More Memorable Milestones 48
Happy First Christmas 50
Happy First Birthday 52
Vacation Time 54
More Special Memories 56

Favorite Things

Your Best Baby Buddies 60
Your Favorite People 62
It's Playtime 64
Let's Sing 66
Let's Read 67
TV Time 68
Activity Time 69
More Special Memories 70

Useful Stuff

Sleeping Log 74
Feeding Log 78
Weight Log 82
Weaning Log 84
Teething Log 86
Immunizations 88
Visits to the Doctor 90
New Friends 92

Notes 94
From Me to You 96

Welcome To The World

FIRST PHOTO OF YOU

Your Name ....

Date of Birth ....

Time You Were Born ....

Where You Were Born ....

FIRST FAMILY PHOTO

Your Weight ....

Your Length ....

Your Hair Color ....

Who You Looked Like

....

....

....

....

....

....

....

Welcome Home

Where You Live

Who Lives With You

Memories of Your First Day at Home

Memories of Your First Night at Home

Who Came to Say Hi

....

....

Special Gifts

....

....

Your Nursery

Special Memories of Your First Weeks

Month-By-Month Memories

Use these pages to record your baby's amazing growth and development in the first year. You'll never tire of looking back at these precious photos and notes.

1 Month Old

Your Weight ....

What You Can Do

....

2 Months Old

Your Weight ....

What You Can Do

....

....

....

....

....

....

....

3 Months Old

Your Weight ....

What You Can Do

4 MONTHS OLD

YOUR WEIGHT ....

WHAT YOU CAN DO

....

....

....

....

....

....

....

5 Months Old

Your Weight ....

What You Can Do

....

....

....

....

....

....

....

6 Months Old

Your Weight ....

What You Can Do

....

....

....

....

....

....

....

7 Months Old

Your Weight ....

What You Can Do

....

....

....

....

....

....

....

8 Months Old

Your Weight ....

What You Can Do

....

....

....

....

....

....

....

9 Months Old

Your Weight ....

What You Can Do

....

....

....

....

....

....

....

10 Months Old

Your Weight ....

What You Can Do

....

....

....

....

....

....

....

11 Months Old

Your Weight ....

What You Can Do

....

....

....

....

....

....

....

12 Months Old

Your Weight ....

What You Can Do

....

....

....

....

....

....

....

Your Tiny Hands

Your Handprint Aged 1 Month...

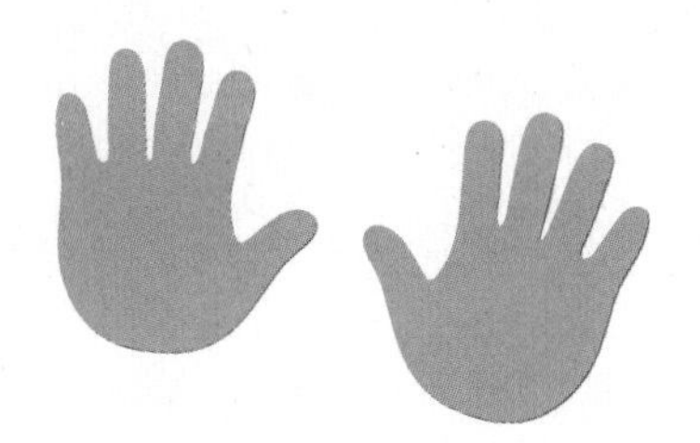

YOUR HANDPRINT AGED 1 YEAR...

YOUR TINY FEET

YOUR FOOTPRINT AGED 1 MONTH...

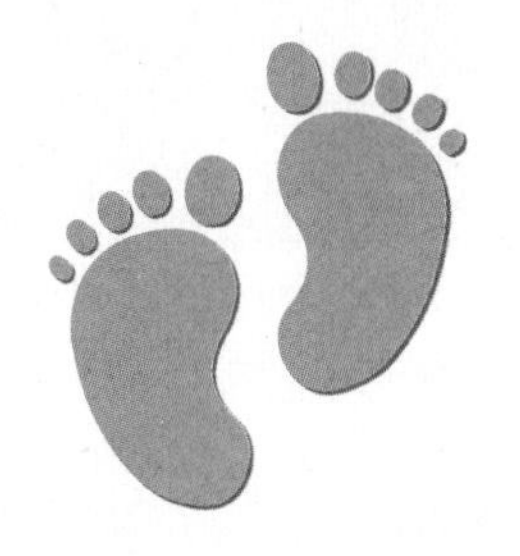

YOUR FOOTPRINT AGED 1 YEAR...

SPECIAL MEMORIES OF YOUR FIRST YEAR

Special Firsts

It's so wonderful when a baby reaches another milestone, from that precious first smile to those first tentative steps. Use these pages to record your photos and memories—not forgetting your baby's all-important first birthday and first Christmas.

It's Bathtime!

Date of Your First Bath..........

Where You Were Bathed..........

Who Bathed You..........

My Memories

Bath Toys You Loved

SEE YOU LATER ...

DATE OF YOUR FIRST OUTING ....

WHERE WE WENT

....

....

....

....

....

....

YOUR FIRST OUTING

The Weather That Day

Who Came With Us

My Memories

Say Cheese!

Date You First Smiled ....

Who/What Made You Smile ....

....

Date You First Laughed..

Who/What Made You Laugh..

....

Your Beautiful Smile

People and Things That Made You Happy

Time For Lunch?

Your First Solid Food

Date You Ate It

Your Age

My Memories

Foods You Loved

Foods You Hated

You can also fill in the weaning log on pages 84–85.

On the Move...

Date You First Rolled Over..

Your Age..

Where You Were

....

....

....

....

....

Date You First Crawled..

Your Age..

Where You Were

....

....

....

....

....

My Memories

You've Got Teeth

Date Your First Tooth Came Through..

Your Age..

Which Tooth Was It?..

Tooth One

TOOTH TWO

Date Your Second Tooth Came Through...

Your Age...

Which Tooth Was It?..

You can also fill in the teething chart on pages 86–87.

Stepping Out

Date You First walked ....

Your Age..

Where You Were

....

....

....

....

....

....

My Memories

FIRST SHOES

More Memorable Milestones

Date You First Sat Unaided.................................Your Age...............................

Date You First Pointed...Your Age...............................

Date You First Clapped...Your Age...............................

Date You First Waved Bye-bye..............................Your Age...............................

YOUR FIRST WORD WAS..........

DATE.......... YOUR AGE..........

OTHER EARLY WORDS

HAPPY FIRST CHRISTMAS!

WHERE YOU SPENT CHRISTMAS

WHO WAS THERE

Your First Stocking Contained...

Your First Gifts From Santa Were...

HAPPY 1ST BIRTHDAY!

WHAT WE DID ON YOUR 1ST BIRTHDAY

Who Was There

Special First Birthday Gifts

VACATION TIME!

DATE OF YOUR FIRST VACATION ....

WHERE WE WENT..

....

HOW WE GOT THERE..

....

What We Did

More Special Memories

Favorite Things

It's so easy to forget the small details of the first year. Use these pages to note down the things your baby loved the most, such as favorite songs and beloved books, and the weekly activities you enjoyed together.

YOUR BEST BABY BUDDIES

NAME ....

BIRTHDAY ....

NAME ....

BIRTHDAY ....

YOUR BUDDY ....

NAME ....

BIRTHDAY ....

NAME ....

BIRTHDAY ....

YOU CAN NOTE DOWN ALL THE NEW FRIENDS
YOU AND YOUR BABY HAVE MADE
ON PAGES 92–93.

YOUR BUDDY..

YOUR FAVORITE PEOPLE

SPECIAL FAMILY

Special Friends

It's Play Time!

Favorite Toy

Who Gave It To You

YOU ALSO LOVED PLAYING WITH...

Let's Sing!

Favorite Songs

Favorite Nursery Rhymes

Let's Read

Favorite Books

TV Time

Favorite TV Shows

Favorite Characters

Activity Time

Group/Club..

What We Did There..

....

Who We Met..

....

Group/Club..

What We Did There..

....

Who We Met..

....

Group/Club..

What We Did There..

....

Who We Met..

....

....

....

More Special Memories

Useful Stuff

Stay organized and keep track of your baby's everyday care with easy-to-use feeding and sleeping logs. Fill in the medical pages to keep a useful record of your baby's health.

Sleeping Log

By keeping a record of your baby's sleep, you will see a pattern emerge and, from that, be able to establish naptime and bedtime routines. Photocopy these pages, if necessary, to build up a longer sleep record. Be aware that your baby's sleep may be affected by many things, such as growth spurts, illness, and even the weather.

Week Beginning...

	Nighttime	Morning	Afternoon	Total Sleep in 24 Hours
Monday				
Tuesday				
Wednesday				
Thursday				
Friday				
Saturday				
Sunday				

Week Beginning...

	Nighttime	Morning	Afternoon	Total Sleep in 24 Hours
Monday				
Tuesday				
Wednesday				
Thursday				
Friday				
Saturday				
Sunday				

Week Beginning...

	Nighttime	Morning	Afternoon	Total Sleep in 24 Hours
Monday				
Tuesday				
Wednesday				
Thursday				
Friday				
Saturday				
Sunday				

Week beginning...

	Nighttime	Morning	Afternoon	Total Sleep in 24 Hours
Monday				
Tuesday				
Wednesday				
Thursday				
Friday				
Saturday				
Sunday				

WEEK BEGINNING..

	NIGHTTIME	MORNING	AFTERNOON	TOTAL SLEEP IN 24 HOURS
MONDAY				
TUESDAY				
WEDNESDAY				
THURSDAY				
FRIDAY				
SATURDAY				
SUNDAY				

WEEK BEGINNING..

	NIGHTTIME	MORNING	AFTERNOON	TOTAL SLEEP IN 24 HOURS
MONDAY				
TUESDAY				
WEDNESDAY				
THURSDAY				
FRIDAY				
SATURDAY				
SUNDAY				

WEEK BEGINNING...

	NIGHTTIME	MORNING	AFTERNOON	TOTAL SLEEP IN 24 HOURS
MONDAY				
TUESDAY				
WEDNESDAY				
THURSDAY				
FRIDAY				
SATURDAY				
SUNDAY				

WEEK BEGINNING...

	NIGHTTIME	MORNING	AFTERNOON	TOTAL SLEEP IN 24 HOURS
MONDAY				
TUESDAY				
WEDNESDAY				
THURSDAY				
FRIDAY				
SATURDAY				
SUNDAY				

Feeding Log

In the early days, it may feel as if you are feeding all the time. Keeping a note of when and for how long your baby feeds can help you to establish some sort of routine if you want to, although you may prefer to feed on demand. There are columns for breastfeeding and bottlefeeding—you may be doing a combination of both. For breastfeeding, it can help to keep a note of which breast you fed from. Photocopy these pages, if necessary, to build up a longer feeding record.

Date	Time Fed	How Long (breast)	Amount (bottle)

DATE	TIME FED	HOW LONG (BREAST)	AMOUNT (BOTTLE)

DATE	TIME FED	HOW LONG (BREAST)	AMOUNT (BOTTLE)

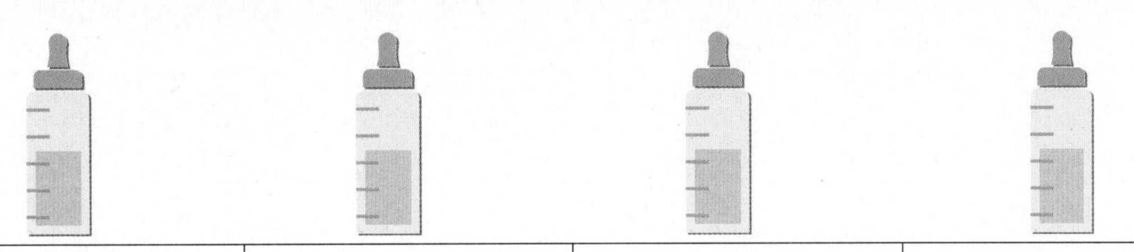

DATE	TIME FED	HOW LONG (BREAST)	AMOUNT (BOTTLE)

Weight Log

Your healthcare providers will regularly weigh your baby in the first few months, but you may want to keep your own record on these pages. The percentile, which is a guide to your baby's growth compared to other babies the same age, can be found in the growth charts provided by your midwife. However, you only need to be concerned if there is a sudden weight loss or gain. Photocopy these pages, if necessary, to build up a longer weight record.

Date.. Weight..
Age.. Percentile..

Date.. Weight..
Age.. Percentile..

Date.. Weight..
Age.. Percentile..

Date.. Weight..
Age.. Percentile..

Date.. Weight..
Age.. Percentile..

DATE.. WEIGHT..
AGE.. PERCENTILE..

DATE.. WEIGHT..
AGE.. PERCENTILE..

DATE.. WEIGHT..
AGE.. PERCENTILE..

DATE.. WEIGHT..
AGE.. PERCENTILE..

DATE.. WEIGHT..
AGE.. PERCENTILE:..

DATE.. WEIGHT..
AGE.. PERCENTILE...............................

DATE.. WEIGHT....................................
AGE.. PERCENTILE...............................

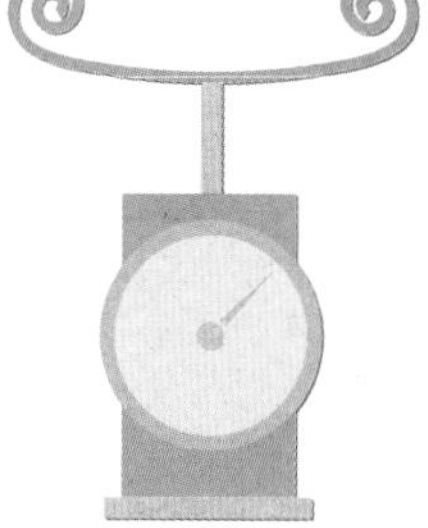

WEANING LOG

When weaning your baby, start slowly with simple purées and soft finger foods and remember that in the early days you are just establishing taste and texture—breast milk or formula will still be your baby's main food source for some months. There's space below to note down foods you've tried and whether your baby liked them. If your little one doesn't like a food, try it again on a few more occasions.

DATE............................FOOD..LIKE/ DISLIKE

DATE............................FOOD..LIKE/ DISLIKE

DATE............................FOOD..LIKE/ DISLIKE

DATE............................FOOD..LIKE/ DISLIKE

DATE............................FOOD..LIKE/ DISLIKE

DATE............................FOOD..LIKE/ DISLIKE

DATE............................FOOD..LIKE/ DISLIKE

DATE............................FOOD..LIKE/ DISLIKE

DATE............................FOOD..LIKE/ DISLIKE

DATE............................FOOD..LIKE/ DISLIKE

DATE............................FOOD..LIKE/ DISLIKE

DATE............................FOOD..LIKE/ DISLIKE

DATE............................FOOD..LIKE/ DISLIKE

DATE............................FOOD..LIKE/ DISLIKE

Favorite Recipes

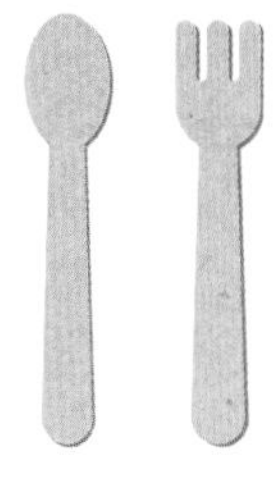

Once weaning is established, you'll begin to make proper balanced meals for your baby. Note down those that seemed to get a thumbs-up!

Recipe..

Source..

....

Recipe..

Source..

....

Recipe..

Source..

....

Recipe..

Source..

....

Recipe..

Source..

....

Teething Log

Make a note of the date and age your baby's teeth come through in the chart opposite, and tick them off on the diagram below. Teeth tend to come through in pairs and the numbers below indicate the order in which this usually occurs.

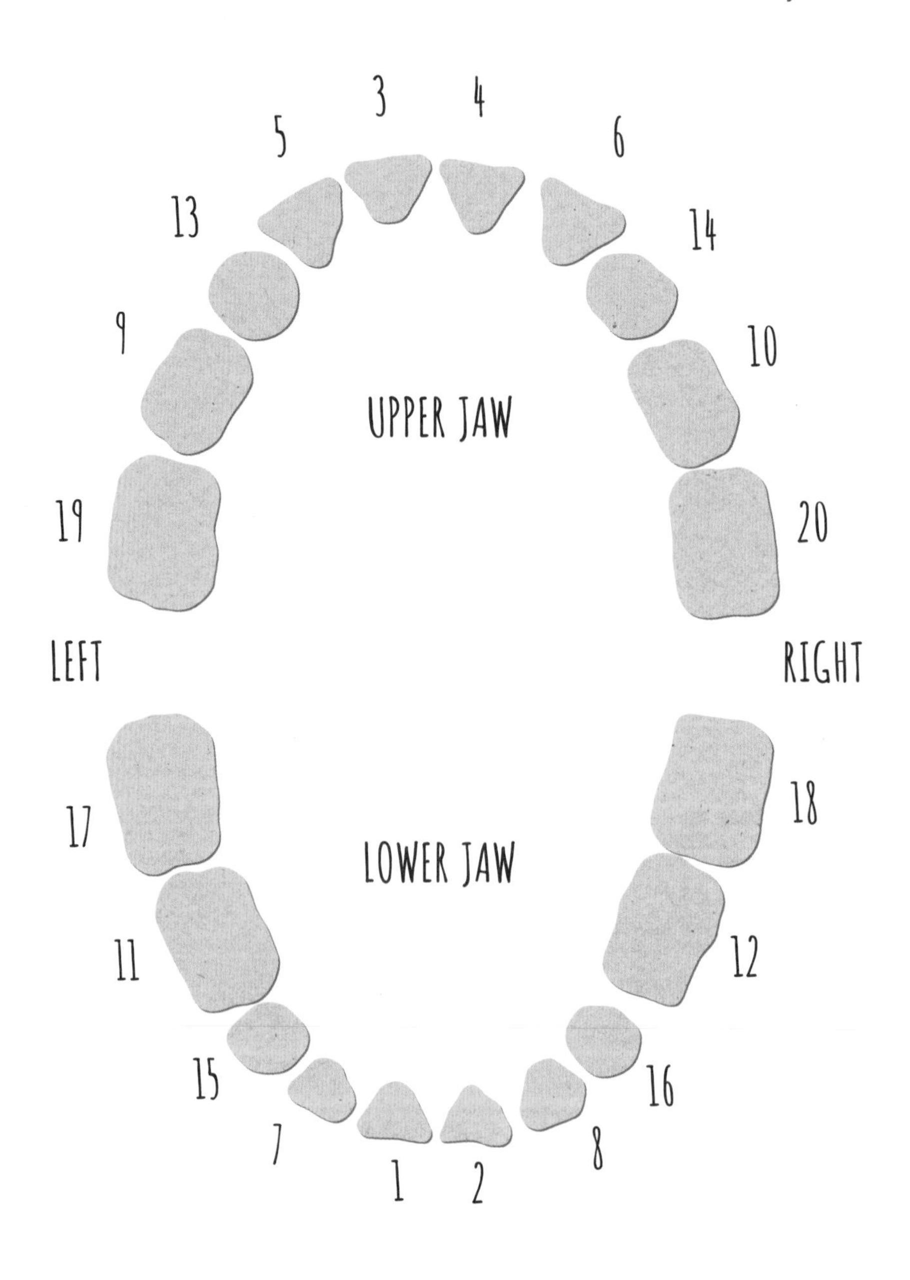

	Date	Age
Tooth 1		
Tooth 2		
Tooth 3		
Tooth 4		
Tooth 5		
Tooth 6		
Tooth 7		
Tooth 8		
Tooth 9		
Tooth 10		
Tooth 11		
Tooth 12		
Tooth 13		
Tooth 14		
Tooth 15		
Tooth 16		
Tooth 17		
Tooth 18		
Tooth 19		
Tooth 20		

IMMUNIZATIONS

It is recommended that all babies have routine immunizations to protect them from potentially serious illnesses. Use these pages to keep an immunization record.
If you are concerned about any aspects of immunization and possible side-effects, seek advice from your healthcare provider.

DATE..

AGE..

IMMUNIZATIONS..

....

SIDE-EFFECTS (IF ANY)..................................

....

....

....

DATE..

AGE..

IMMUNIZATIONS..

....

SIDE-EFFECTS (IF ANY)..................................

....

....

....

DATE..

AGE..

IMMUNIZATIONS..

....

SIDE-EFFECTS (IF ANY)..................................

....

....

....

DATE..

AGE..

IMMUNIZATIONS..

....

SIDE-EFFECTS (IF ANY)..

....

....

....

DATE..

AGE..

IMMUNIZATIONS..

....

SIDE-EFFECTS (IF ANY)..

....

....

....

DATE..

AGE..

IMMUNIZATIONS..

....

SIDE-EFFECTS (IF ANY)..

....

....

....

DATE..

AGE..

IMMUNIZATIONS..

....

SIDE-EFFECTS (IF ANY)..

....

....

....

Visits to the Doctor

It can be useful to keep a record of your baby's visits to the doctor, not least so that you can spot if a condition is recurring and note how often your baby has had a particular medication, such as antibiotics.

Date...

Symptoms...

Doctor...

Diagnosis..

Treatment...

Date...

Symptoms...

Doctor...

Diagnosis..

Treatment...

Date...

Symptoms...

Doctor...

Diagnosis..

Treatment...

DATE..

SYMPTOMS..

DOCTOR..

DIAGNOSIS...

TREATMENT..

DATE..

SYMPTOMS..

DOCTOR..

DIAGNOSIS...

TREATMENT..

DATE..

SYMPTOMS..

DOCTOR..

DIAGNOSIS...

TREATMENT..

New Friends

You'll meet a lot of other parents through having a baby, and their children are likely to become your baby's buddies. Use these pages to note down the names and contact details of your new social circle.

Name.. Child's name..

Where Met.. Phone Number..

Name.. Child's name..

Where Met.. Phone Number..

Name.. Child's name..

Where Met.. Phone Number..

Name.. Child's name..

Where Met.. Phone Number..

Name.. Child's name..

Where Met.. Phone Number..

Name.. Child's name..

Where Met.. Phone Number..

Name.. Child's name..

Where Met... Phone Number...

Name.. Child's name..

Where Met... Phone Number...

Name.. Child's name..

Where Met... Phone Number...

Name.. Child's name..

Where Met... Phone Number...

Name.. Child's name..

Where Met... Phone Number...

Name.. Child's name..

Where Met... Phone Number...

Notes

From Me to You

Use this final page to write a letter to your child expressing what this first year of parenthood has meant to you. It will be a letter that your child can treasure forever.